MIND ON MY MONEY!!!

A Thinking Man's Journal on Money Matters

LAWRENCE A. GHOLSON II

MAX Publishing, LLC

**LAWRENCE A.
GHOLSON III**

Mind On My Money!

Published by MAX Publishing, LLC

Published in the United States of America.

ISBN-13: 978-1-970097-09-2

Disclaimer/Warning:

This book is intended for lecture and educational purposes only.

This program provides no guarantees of effectiveness for ALL Persons. This book is the opinion of the writer and serves as a guide to support the lecture or training offered by the writer and team.

Book cover illustrations (front and back) by Trevor Lucas

Book Cover photography by Raymond Paige

Editor: Alesha Brown LLC

DEDICATION

I simply dedicate this workbook to you, man, with one simple request:

Share what you learn with every man, young and old.

Allow the tools I share in this book to be a conversation starter. More importantly, may this spark a lifelong conversation that results in you having your mind on your money and your money on your mind!

Table of Contents

MIND ON MY MONEY!!!

A Thinking Man's Journal on Money Matters

THIS BOOK IS FOR:

- The **everyday man** who has struggled with managing money.
- Every man who desires to be financially free FOR REAL.
- Every man desiring to not just work hard, but desiring to work smarter in understanding and applying practical principles to cash flow planning.

YOU are the "everyday man" if…:

- … You weren't taught about financial literacy.
- … You only knew money was scarce as a child (never seemed to be enough) or that somehow the bills were paid.
- … You don't just want the finer things in life, but you have a desire to always have more than enough (passive income).
- … You want to enhance what you're currently doing with your money.

1. Pocket Lent to Pocket Change

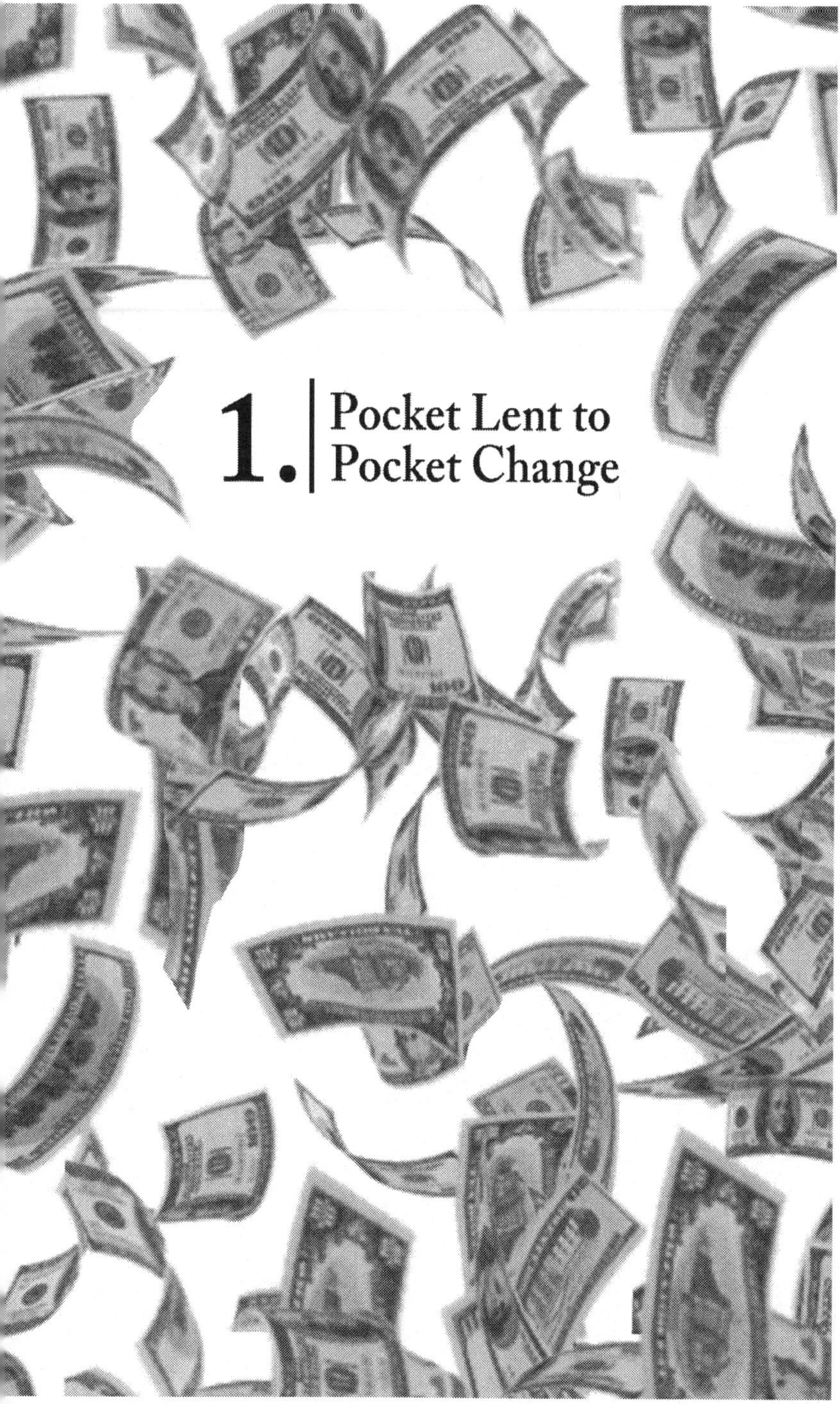

MIND ON MY MONEY!!!

A Thinking Man's Journal on Money Matters

This workbook is more of a tool to help you think about what you really want to accomplish with your money. It is not a magic potion where you quote it and things just appear.

This conversation or experience will require work on your part. You may find that most of the work required is mental: you must first change your mindset or "unlearn" some stuff to make room for practical growth.

You will find nuggets throughout these pages revealing how I overcame similar challenges, but I am not encouraging you to be a *carbon copy* of me. I can't guarantee that if you do exactly what I have done that you will get the exact same results. Honestly, no one can because we are all individuals and have different needs and desires on which drives our success and results.

However, I can guarantee that if you apply the principles, techniques and mindset that this guide teaches you and your family's financial lives will forever be transformed. I can assure you that if you strategically apply the information shared here, you will have more than you need to help you better manage your funds.

Think of this guide as a conversation between you and me: a straightforward, real talk conversation about what has worked for me, what has not worked for me and what has and has not worked for you along the journey of minding our money, maaaan.

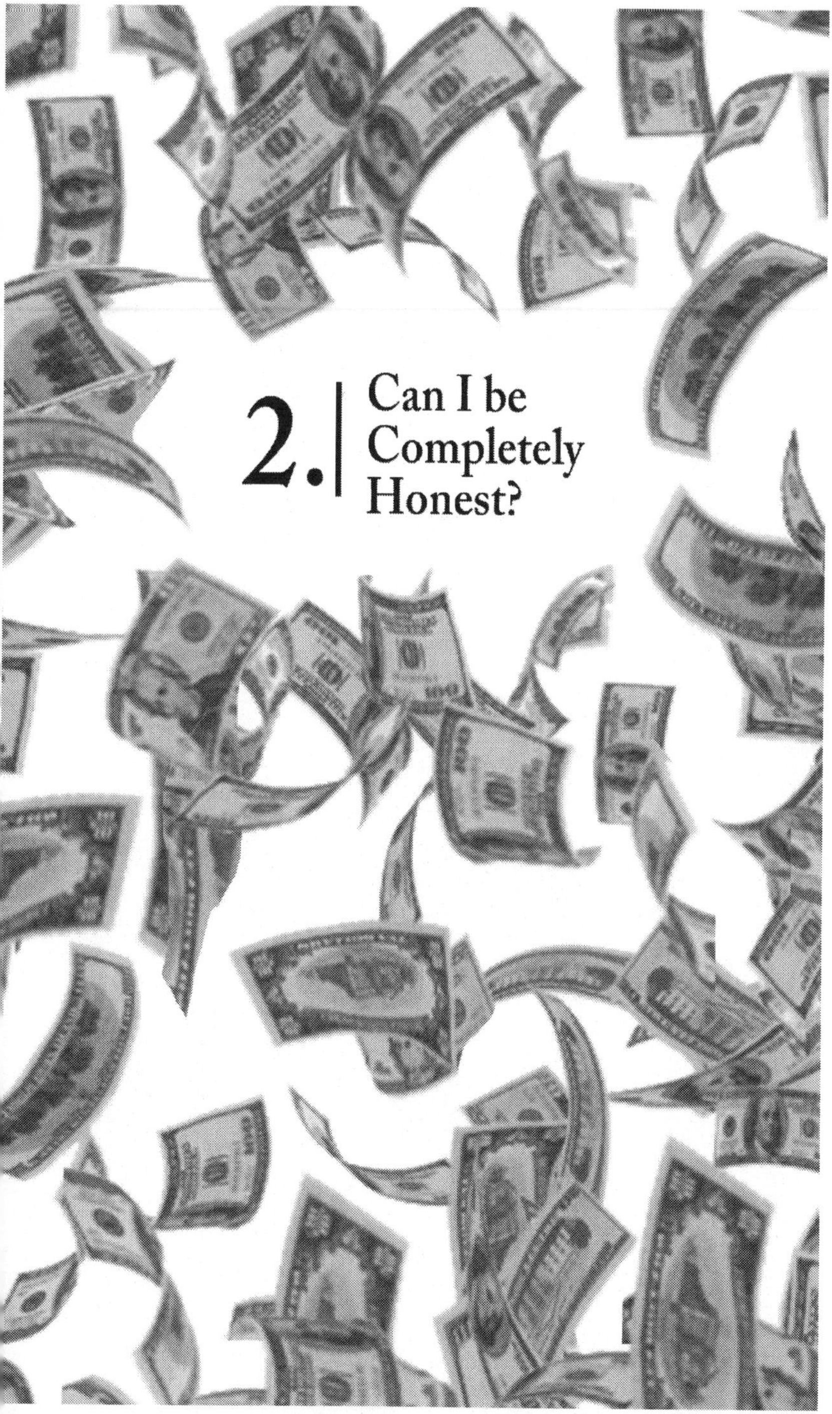

2. Can I be Completely Honest?

Listen, can I be completely real with you here? Of course I can!

Many women assume that we [men] don't ask enough questions when it comes to anything, from simple driving directions to reading diagrams or assembly instructions. But, fellas, we know the real truth, don't we?

Men, we are equally–if not more so–as inquisitive, investigative and rationally astute as women. (I know there is some woman reading this book so, since I've spilled the beans, let me drop the other half of this truth bomb and end this once and for all.) Men are equally as inquisitive, investigative and rationally astute as women when … it comes to something **we find VALUE in**.

Talk to a man about his favorite sports team, his favorite muscle car, the latest in gun collections or fishing and hunting gear. Better yet, talk to a man about the best-compounded workout to build massive biceps and triceps or maybe even what current real estate deals yield the highest ROI (return on investment).

Women, if you try any of these, be prepared

For the hours of historical data and comparisons he will share. At the very least, you will walk away with a working knowledge to contribute to a decent conversation on that subject matter, *if you listen*. (Point proved, so I'm going to go back to my dialogue with my men and, hopefully, the man in your life.)

"Mr. Gholson, it's Steve, your Service Technician!"

Steve is the friendly guy at my new auto servicing location. Today is my first official maintenance visit for my 6.2-liter V8 engine 4WD Crew Cab Pick Up Truck.

Man, I love my truck! It has become a great conversation piece in my community among the guys. With a commanding 420+ horsepower, it handles rough terrain like a champ while providing luxury appeal!

Being that it is the first time the service

department would be handling my truck, Steve wanted to make sure I knew that they would have to build a history regardless of my paperwork detailing all the previous maintenance work. Although I brought my truck in for the 50,000-mile maintenance check, I previously had other things checked or changed out completely. (Guys, you know how we do our after-factory upgrades.)

Steve and the company wanted to make sure I didn't have unnecessary costs for suggested maintenance work that I already had. (As one who keeps my mind on my money, I definitely appreciated their honesty.)

Steve's honesty makes him "the friendly nice guy", but it is ultimately my responsibility and accountability to know my vehicle's needs. Remember, Steve is also in the business to make MONEY–the power of suggestion is real. How else can you go in for a basic oil change and be terrified by a list of unexpected things that are potentially problematic with your car?

There is no coincidence that even if you don't buy into your auto technician's maintenance suggestions, you leave somewhat scared to drive home. Can you relate?

(TIP: If you apply the proper mindset, you will turn these times into learning opportunities that provide you with a working knowledge of your automobile, its maintenance schedule and needs.)

Now, you could care less about my trip to the service department, but I needed you to see how easily that rolled off my tongue. Fellas, I bet most of you understood it as if we spoke a language unique to men only! (If you listen to the women in your life, we do.)

Well, I am here to tell you that money has a similar language and, guess what fellas, we speak it! I know, it blew my mind initially too!

So, when we talk about *pulling our credit report*, we are simply saying it's time to *get your inspection* done! If you are anything like me, word associations are the best! I figured we may be a lot alike if you are investing your time in reading this workbook. We simply want to know how to get things done in the most sensible, efficient and practical way possible.

Does security matter to men as much as it matters to women? Candidly, from my research for many men, our general concerns for security is attached to the women in our lives and usually surrounds these women throughout our lives.

For example, it's usually the woman you love who has the "dream house" in mind or the vision of the destination trips and vacations. Through that woman, the idea of family becomes a consideration and, before you know it, children may be added to the equation. Of course, with all of this comes a plethora of security needs to invade the man's mind and ultimately his decision-making habits (hope-fully).

The essence of life is relationships.

The essence of living is those lessons you've learned, usually by way of those relationships.

As men, we are driven to provide, which is directly connected to our ego. Therefore, when I mention Credit Rating and Credit Report, it is foreign to the average man. Not because we don't understand it, but because it hasn't been a factor in our money focus. But, men, it should be a consideration at the very base level.

I will share some practical terms, examples, and scenarios in this workbook to make basic money minding tips come to life for you. (At least, that's my goal.)

Where there are questions, I want you to pause and think about your answer. There is space in this book for you to write your answers, which I encourage you to do! Write all over it–use highlighters, dog ear pages–do all of that if it helps! I also encourage you to get a regular pocket notebook–maybe 3 x 5 or 5 x 8–and record your answers and teachable moments. If you do, you are sort of writing your own version of this book to make it real for you!

If you don't mind, I am going to associate financial terms to automobile maintenance terms. For us men, it gives a different understanding of financial terms and makes it real.

3. Check Your Engine

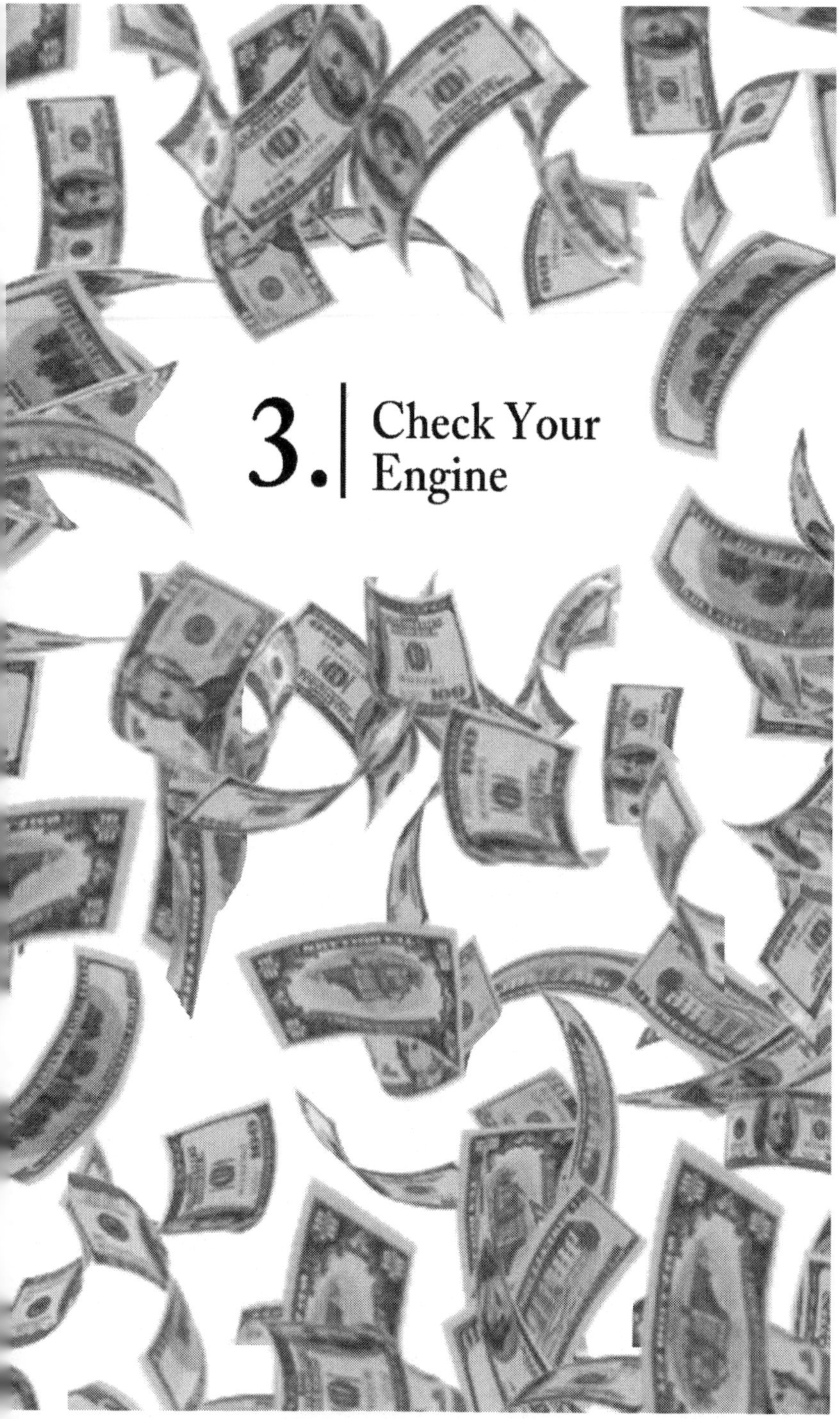

AUTOMOBILE TERM	MONEY TERM
Annual Inspection	Credit Report
Carfax Report	Net Worth/ Financial Statement
Routine Oil Change	Quarterly Wealth Strategies
Tune Up/Maintenance	Financial Goals
GPS	Where you are & where you intend to go The time, miles and detours to consider
Check Engine Light	Regular notifications to consider from CPA/ Estate Planning Attorney/ Tax Advisors/ Financial Advisors/ Banker

Now, I'm hoping that quick reference chart sort of provided you with a practical blueprint for a few important money terms you should have already encountered. Below, you will see those terms hopefully explained in a way that makes it relevant to the basics of money talk! Here goes:

CREDIT REPORT

- ✓ This is like your school report card. Your "grade point average" is the infamous **Credit Score**. Let's just say it's where you get to see if you have an ***A B C D E or F*** based on how you pay those you owe [creditors].

- ✓ The credit report is simply a very detailed list of how your credit "grade" was determined – and let me tell you, it is not as simple as a pass or fail. If you plan on establishing yourself in life, you want to pass this one with a pretty decent grade.

Credit Bureaus track your habits of paying back your lenders. They are less concerned about your spending, but that does not mean you shouldn't be! If your current grade is not that "great", there are practical steps to repair your credit, starting with a conversation/ relationship with your banker.

FINANCIAL STATEMENT

- ✓ It feels like financial documents show up everywhere, right!? If receiving or spending money is involved, you are part of a financial transaction which means a financial statement is soon to follow.
- ✓ A financial statement is an official account of your money activities. This is where you are able to figure out what you are really worth opposed to that number on your check stub that never seems to make it to your hands! (The official term is GROSS pay.)

The professional who compiles this will use the term Balance Sheet, which captures your Assets (what you own and their value); your Liabilities (what you owe including penalties and interest) and, obviously, this determines how much YOU really are worth or your Net

Worth. (When discussing finances or money, be prepared to hear the term NET WORTH often.)

- ✓ Financial statements alone are very important learning tools for keeping your mind on your money.

WEALTH STRATEGIES

- ✓ This is when you are intentionally protecting your current money while planning a structure to acquire additional money (passive income, streams of revenue or MONEY to meet your "wants and emergency funds list").

- ✓ In other words, disciplining your money management, or spending and saving habits, so you can meet the financial goals you set in place for your 'quality of life' plans.

- ✓ You can do the basics yourself, but I highly suggest you meet with a team of professionals to help you meet your money goals. This team would mostly consist of a tax advisor and or a certified public accountant (CPA).

- ✓ If your tax advisor and CPA are not the same person, make sure they communicate with each other on a regular basis. Your team of financial professionals should also include an estate planning attorney and a financial advisor.

- ✓ If any of this is like a foreign language to you, please reread the information and Google it so you will better understand the roles and benefits of these very important people.

FINANCIAL GOALS

Man, What You Gonna Do With Your Money!!?

- ✓ What does it cost for you to live at the level you desire? (Refer back to your *living expenses*.)
- ✓ What new opportunities (like travel, professional development, investments or businesses and partnerships) would you like to explore if the finances were there?
- ✓ What are your ideal cash flow plans if you were too old to work at your current level or unable to work due to failing health or injuries? Retirement also falls in this area.

Most people consider the fantasy of retirement, but neglect to consider lifelong implications beyond retirement, such as possible hospitalization and associated costs or mortgage expense. Being alive but terminally ill costs!

- ✓ What are your financial plans for death/burial? How are you securing and protecting your cash flow so that whomever you leave behind can carry on or close out your final response-bilities with reasonable ease?

- ✓ DEFINE your goals and educate yourself through seminars, network-ing and online webinars. Pick a plan of action and STICK to it. It's a waste of time to create financial goals if you are not going to change your current lifestyle choices in order to achieve those goals!

ADVISORY WINNING TEAM

If you plan on being successful with the money you make or acquire, you will need a winning team around you. You will not need to see or speak to these people every day, but they are key to your money success. You will, however, need to meet with them annually and I would suggest adding a mid-year meeting for good measure. During these two occasions, I find it best to get them all in the same room. After all, your financial advisors need to hear your money goals in order to best advise you.

Now don't get nervous: if you don't have your winning team on Day 1, you need to at least consider them from Day 1! Day 365 is too late!

Who should be a part of your winning advisory team? Please include the following:

- Tax Advisor
- CPA
- Estate Planning Attorney
- Financial Advisor
- Banker

I am used to hearing people say, "But Lawrence, you must be freakin' kiddin' me! I can't afford these guys!" My response is always the same:

> *In the beginning, I thought I couldn't either, but once I received this assnormous* tax bill in the third year of my business, I realized I couldn't afford not to!*

Remember, your winning advisory financial team is your check engine team! Besides, you will find their fees are generally minor once you have established a relationship with them–an authentic relationship where you make a plan based on their advice that you pay for and you follow that plan. Quality people will work with you and with a reasonable budget, from my experience. (*And, yes, I did say *assnormous*!)

No worries—we all may get a Check Engine light from time to time. The key is to address it immediately to avoid problems that will cost you. It may cost you a little now or it may cost you a lot, but it will certainly cost you if you fail to pay attention to the diagnostic warnings that come along your journey.

Who you are now is who you were meant to be.

How you are now is how you choose to be.

---

start engine

Where are you now?

My income from my primary job is: $____

I have additional income from:

1 ____________________

2 ____________________

3 ____________________

(*Additional income* includes any part-time gigs, child support, speaking engagements, trust funds, selling veggies, handyman jobs, side-eye hustles, cleaning, car detailing, door dashing, etc.)

My TOTAL Income each month is: $____

Let's shift Gears into *DRIVE*!

My rent/mortgage is: $__

My power/electric bill averages: $__

My gas bill averages: $__

My water bill averages: $__
(This bill may come every other month, but average it monthly on paper.)

My sanitation bill is: $__

My Me Acct: $__

(*Self Rewards- this one is necessary yet is a flexible expense when budgeted correctly.*)

My cable/internet bill is: $__

My cell phone bill is: $__

My grocery bill averages: $__

Is there alimony or child support? $___

Is it automatically deducted?

MIND ON MY MONEY!!!

A Thinking Man's Journal on Money Matters

Do I have enough $
to make ends meet?

If not, what are some
ways I can INCREASE my
Income

and

DECREASE my *Expenses*?

My transportation: $__

Car Payment/Lease	$
Auto Insurance	$
Uber/Lyft average	$
Fuel	$
Oil Change*	$
Other Maintenance Tires Tune Up	$
Annual Inspection*	$
Vehicle Registration*	$
Roadside Assistance	$
Average Monthly Total	$

*Indicates to average this [amount] into your monthly budget- to keep it simple and to make sure you cover it!

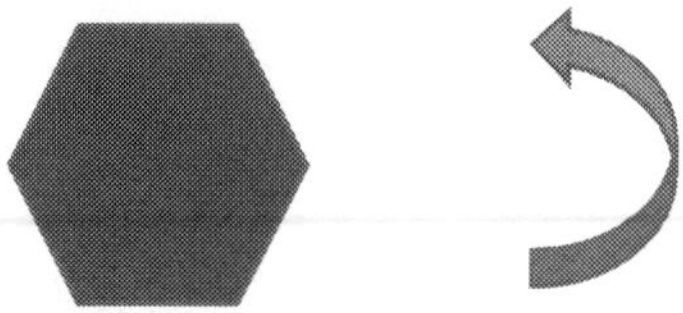

Look back at your numbers in this section.

Honestly, how do you feel about them?

Honestly, why do you feel this way?

***THINK OUT LOUD–no, really, *SAY IT* so that <u>YOU</u> hear it!!**

4. NOW Say Delayed Gratification

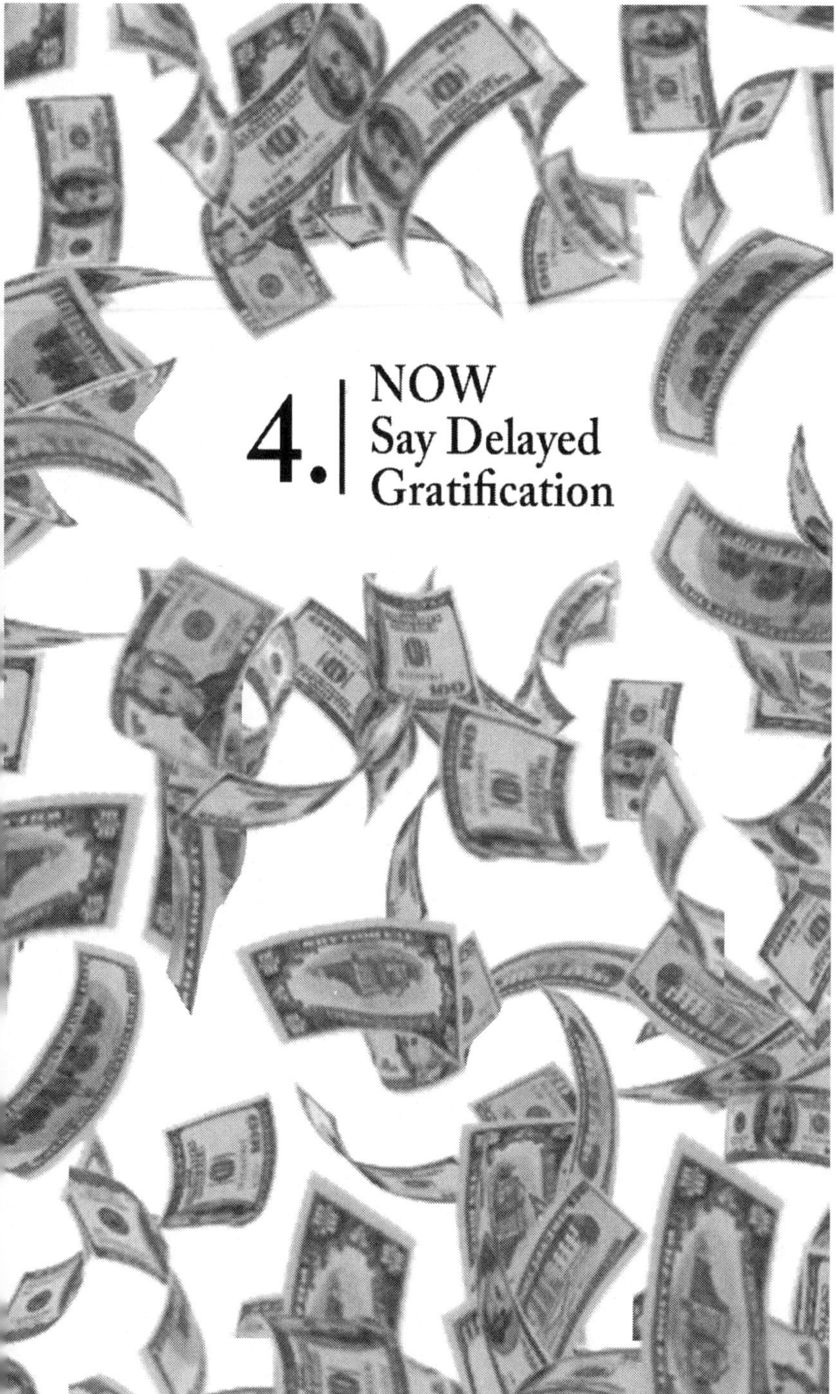

Delayed Gratification

What a harsh thought to some.

What do you mean I may have to wait?

But I want what I want NOW!

Let's consider NOT *living our best lives* **on credit** for a moment! Let's consider NOT confusing our WANTS with our NEEDS for a moment!

You see, I haven't even touched on the latest Js or designer sunshades or that high-end watch, those nice wheels for your car or that *must have* fragrance that gets the ladies' attention. I left alone those cigars with the smooth leaf that pairs well with the top shelf liquor that we must have while seated in the VIP section overlooking the crowd somewhere. For a moment, let's consider DELAYED GRATIFICATION!

When folks ask me how I acquired my current financial freedom– (and I am still on the path to my ideal) –I tell them that I had to wait for some things. I started where I was, used what I had and did what I could until I could do more! And once I could do more, I DID!

The very idea of saving and waiting tends to send many of my clients' anxiety level way up. I can tell it right away. There's the wrinkle in the middle of the forehead or the fine beads of sweat starting just near the edge of the hairline. Then there are all those undeniable nonverbal cues while the client is doing their best award-winning performance, which is often quite impressive, to remain calm and chill. And it's at this very moment that I allow the silence in the room to take charge.

Most people don't want to do that because we live in a society of *right now*. Credit makes it so easy for us to buy now, pay later.

Living our lives this way puts us at financial risk.

With no thought of the unpredictable circumstances life can throw our way–like waking up one day to a government shutdown, losing a job, the inability to compete in a changing industry or health issues preventing you from maintaining work or 1 even a government shut-down–our world shatters.

The real question is: *Are we willing to delay our wants NOW to secure our future world?*

Will YOU delay your WANTS for your future?

MIND ON MY MONEY!!!

A Thinking Man's Journal on Money Matters

What's on your *I NEED RIGHT NOW list* (this is what I call WANTS)?

What are you *really* feeling when you consider that some things could wait until later (delayed gratification)?

____

____

____

____

____

Now let's go back to your list of I NEED RIGHT NOW.

For each item, describe what you would gain if it were delayed.

Must Haves	Benefit of Delay
________________	________________
________________	________________
________________	________________
________________	________________
________________	________________
________________	________________
________________	________________

Thinking About Your Better Future:

Make quick notes here of how you can think differently concerning what your NEEDS truly are versus your NEEDS RIGHT NOW.

Let us visit a couple of line items I deliberately left out earlier. I wanted you to take time to digest your initial liabilities and assets columns–you know, the whole Income/ Expense report.

But I really wanted these line items to stand out in your mind a little more. Far too many people have faced situations impacted by this. I think it is because they didn't consider these line items as a major part of the expense report. On the contrary, fellas, each one is extremely important.

Life Insurance: Death and Burial Expenses

Ask yourself:

Do I have Life Insurance?

And which is the best for my current lifestyle? (Look up or inquire about the definitions for the following terms and consider your personal knowledge and make comparisons.)

- ✓ WHOLE LIFE is ____________________

  ____

  ____

- ✓ TERM LIFE is ______________________

  ____

  ____

Have I truly prepared for my Death and Burial? (If you haven't, this becomes an unfair expense for somebody else). How can your loved ones properly grieve with this lingering?

Will I have a funeral? Will I be cremated? How much does this cost? Does my Life

Insurance policy at least cover this expense? (If my last policy is over 30 years old, is it still beneficial to my family needs upon my death?)

Discuss Discuss Discuss

Plan Plan Plan

Document Document Document

Revisit Revisit Revisit

This is big for me as I have personally experienced this with my family. It's not something you want to face or leave your loved ones **unprepared** to face.

What are you feeling right now? Are you willing to stop living the life you have now in order to live the life you want?

Okay, now it's time to really capture our MONEY MOVEMENTS:

My **TOTAL EXPENSES** per month averages: **$__**

My **TOTAL MONTHLY INCOME** (what comes in) **$__**

Minus

My **TOTAL MONTHLY EXPENSES** (what goes out) **$__**

Equals

(*SURPLUS*...this is what you have left)

Income		Expenses		Balance
	=		=	
	=		=	
	=		=	
	=		=	

Now let's discuss credit: uh… NOPE! First, men, can we just OPEN OUR MAIL?!! It does us no good to go straight to credit reports unless we deal with the basics.

5. First of All, Open Your Mail

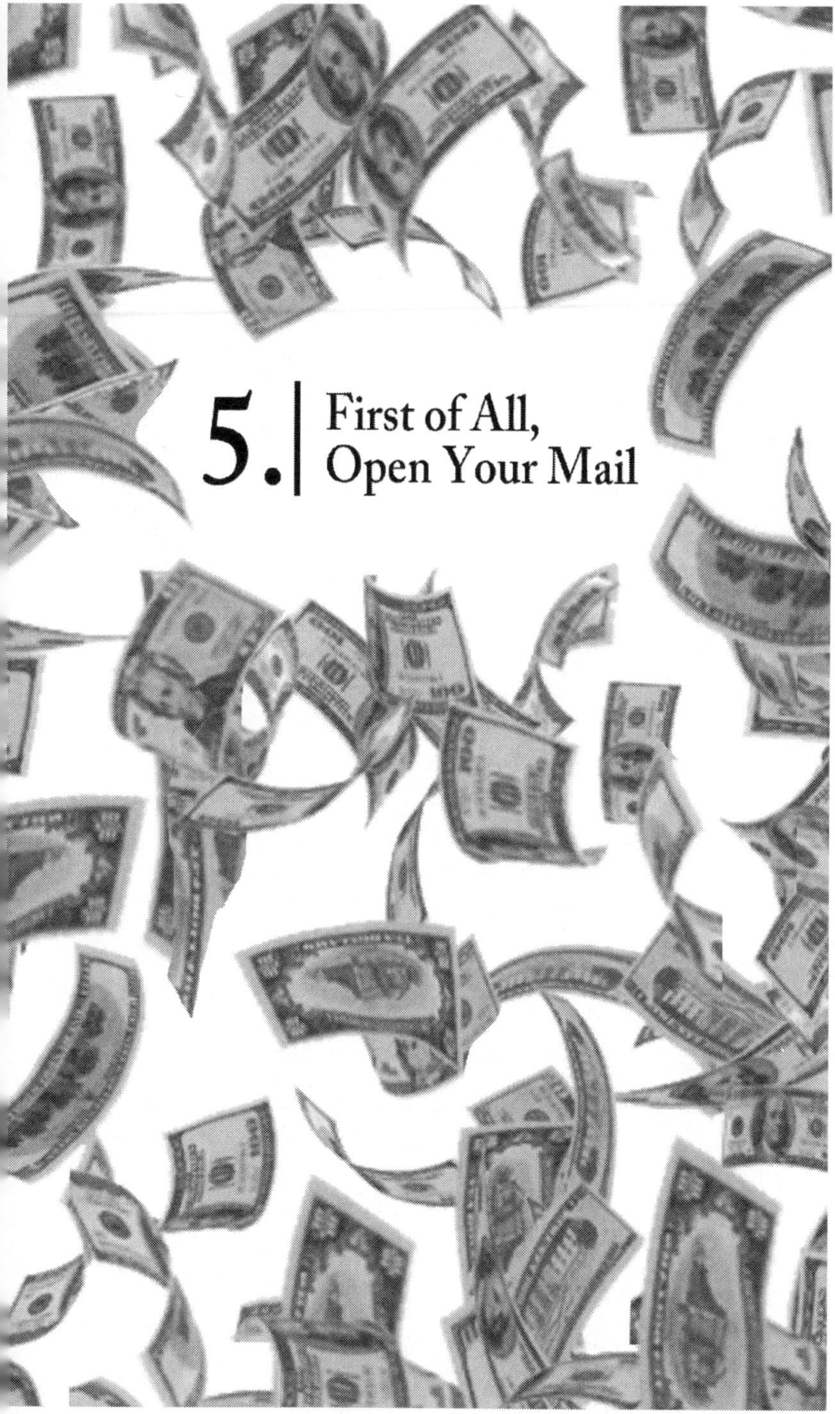

Man, open your mail, dammit! I get it, I get it! My 20s were a lot like this too! Quite honestly, I only opened the mail when it arrived with the nice bold IMMEDIATE ACTION is required label, especially on light bills or other major utility bills like gas and telephone. Remember when they use to put those door hangers on your door, letting you know when they had made a "courtesy" visit?

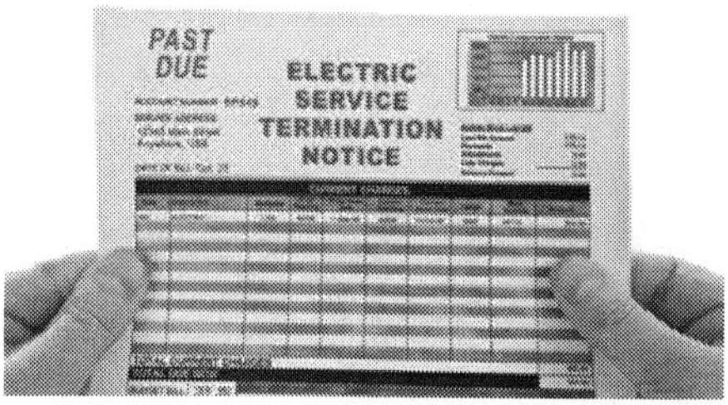

Wait, is that still a thing?! It seemed as if I would I only make a move when my ego was under attack and someone other than me would see the notice or be affected by it. Honestly, I still have a disdain for paying a utility bill down to zero! Don't get me wrong, I enjoy paying three to six months in advance now. I do so just because I know the disdain from those primitive years.

Looking back to my early adult years, I know I experienced anxiety/panic attacks when it came to thinking about my finances. I had moved from taking care of only me, which didn't require much, to the pressures of taking care of a family. The responsibility of having to take care of a family resembled my childhood woes and I HAD TO DO SOMETHING to make sure MY MIND WAS ON MY MONEY!

Eventually, when it came to my panic attacks over money, I had to realize that this was *my* life. I had to make a decision. I chose to come to grips with my fear and anxiety: face it, fight it and defeat it! And, trust me when I say, it can be a beast to reckon with.

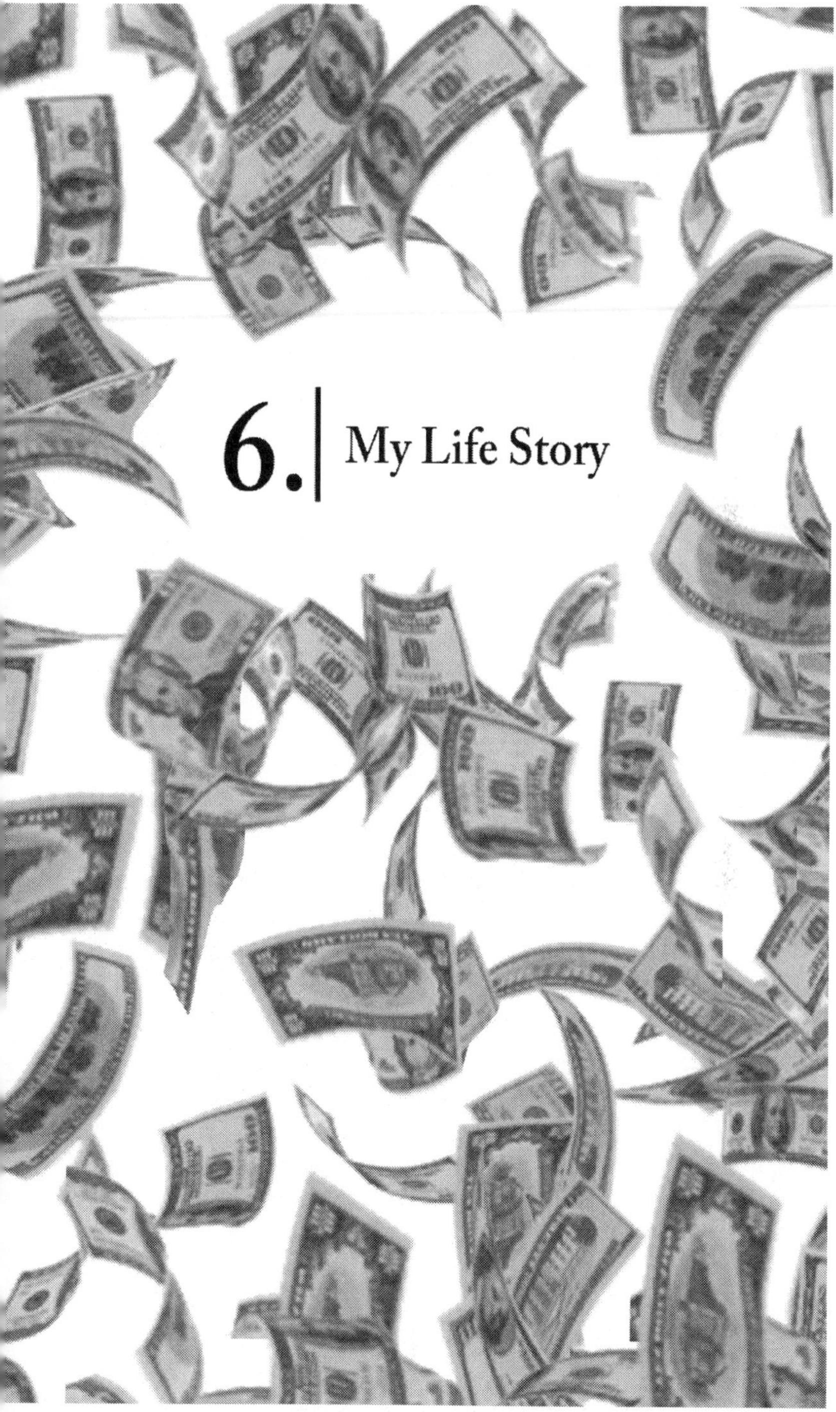

6. My Life Story

MIND ON MY MONEY!!!

A Thinking Man's Journal on Money Matters

I am one of the older children born from the two youngest children of two larger families. My dad is the youngest of 12 and my mom is the youngest of eight. Cute, I know, however, we all know what they say about the “babies” of the family and the associated mindset.

The youngest child of any family typically doesn’t have to deal with the responsibility and pressures of a lot of things their older siblings did, which had an impact on my early learning curves, habits and ultimate goals. Early on, I had an insatiable need to "make money" and to be able to take care of my own. What I missed, though, were those all-important strategies for wealth building and saving.

At seven and a half years old I was getting paid "change" for working on the farm (sharecropping) during the tobacco season. My job was to drive the loading sleigh and guide the horse down the neat span of rows while those “pulling tobacco” stack loaded.

As I grew older, I learned to scale those hot barn walls with Spider-Man precision, in order to stack poles of strung tobacco on flats which were left to cure and dry way up in the top of the barns! But I got PAID!

Chopping firewood, raking leaves, recycling aluminum cans–I did it without issue and with no one really aware of my WHY. You see, when you are wired like I was as a kid and basically never truly exposed to financial planning, (yet overhearing money problems or sensing the bills were always past due), you quickly figure out it's up to you to at least take care of you. Looking back now I realize that my initial education was demonstrated through financial reactions opposed to financial planning! I know now that I was not alone in that classroom. I have mentored and coached many clients who, at the core level, resemble my history.

I'm grateful because my story keeps me relatable, relevant and real! Just writing this I can smell the dusty floors and feel the piping heat from front-loaded wood stoves inside those barn structures! Hell, I can even smell the darkened dry leaves of the cured tobacco. I clearly remember going with my uncle and my granddaddy to the crowded bidding markets to sell the harvest! This time period, I believe, was when I understood that money has a voice!

Thinking back, it was almost as if I could hear money speaking *in stereo*! Yes, I could hear money speaking ALL around me as these men wagered in this crowded open space and myself–seemingly the only little guy in the building. As the "colonel", also known as the auctioneer, enticed the deal with his speedy talking chants, I witnessed the crowd of mostly men frenzy to acquire what they wanted. At that moment, I knew I needed to learn this new language for my life.

Money's voice seemed way too mature for me to know, but the conversation between my granddaddy and his eldest son told me that these wins meant something to our family. Reflecting back, it really was a life lesson that even serves me today and I was always excited when they allowed little old me to tag along!

We must accept the END of something in order to BEGIN something new.

I like sharing all of this information so that you can see a clear picture of how I harnessed this non-traditional education in an effort to become better. (Until now, I really wasn't clearly aware of the value I gained from my trial and error detours and recalibrations, but I hope you find my transparency relatable to your journey. No *silver spoon* here guys; not even running water until I was 14 years old!) I appreciate my story, ALL of my story because it is ME!

I consider my experiences as a front line introduction to *if it's to be then it's up to ME!* Yet, I was still a quiet storm but, trust me, I had my mind on my money. I worked to pay for most things I participated in during school. In no way am I saying I was the first or the only child exposed to this story. In fact, sharing this has been difficult because I never wanted it to come across that my parents weren't providers or great parents. They were great providers and still are great parents, but the times were the times.

MIND ON MY MONEY!!!

A Thinking Man's Journal on Money Matters

I was raised in a rural community and culture where parents did "the best they knew how in order to *make do*." My goal is to build on the wonderful, humble platform my parents lovingly provided. After all, wouldn't it be foolish for me not to push beyond a *make do* moment when it's in my power to push beyond?

My parents will be the first to tell you, as an adult, my transition to *my here* at times has been challenging and frustrating. You see, I still had that little boy inside of me who felt the weight of responsibility and the pressure to make them proud. Inside of me was a quiet storm of brewing frustration to understand–to simply understand.

I watched what appeared to be loved ones settling or fearing life. I am certain I came across weird to some of my folks back then. I thought and responded differently, but we just defined me as "unique". I was a natural born risk taker in learning how to dream BIG until I figured out a way to match those dreams to my reality. I'm still working on it all, but I'm getting better at it all the time!

My thoughts were too much at times for my parents, but I believe it has served me well. Thank God they never discouraged my weird thought process! By the way, one of my simple pleasures still is listening to faucet water. Seriously, I will turn on the faucet and walk away just to hear it in the background. This drives my wife crazy, lol.

You see how all of my experiences would possibly strain financial dialogues between my wife and me? Consider how the adult us impacted the childhood us. Nevertheless, we worked and worked and worked on our issues through and through. Honestly, it was much work and difficult work, but we were committed to pioneer the difference for our family and to change the trajectory of our earth story!

Thank you, my Love, for fighting this battle with me over the years. The extreme planner in my wife and the abstract risk taker in me drew a line in the sand. My wife and I have always stood solid on becoming our progressive best selves. That's not to infer that this has come easily for either one of us, but it has been pretty cool to realize that we understand each other's visions of financial fitness and freedom as well as a simplistic well thought out quality lifestyle!

You see, my young, brilliant girlfriend, now my wife, loved our TV dreams and believed in our magic. We were determined to turn pocket lent into our dynasty. We became our own silver lining to the possibilities! See guys, we always saw us living our full potential! My wife has always been my business magnet mogul!

My grandma had me watching Victor Newman as a young kid. (Victor Newman was the fictional self-made billionaire on one of grandma's favorite "stories", The Young & The Restless.) I was mesmerized by the story, unbeknownst to her. From that single wide mobile home, Victor mentored me and I believed in a lifestyle I had never known. (Let me pause right here and say, **Thank You, Grandma!)**

Mr. Newman, the *Black Knight*, living a life of comfort, respect and admiration filled with a quiet power, could yield like a sword when necessary. I had a goal for the very first time; an undetected superhero.

Imagine my amazement when I discovered my wife watched the same soap opera and dreamt of being Kaye Chancellor, a true and formidable power duchess whom Victor Newman loved, admired and respected! I think I was 10 years old, the age my oldest grandson is now, and my mind was on my money when every other kid was focused on the latest trend.

Write down anything you just read that you relate to:

____

____

____

____

____

You see, I am a believer that we are more alike than we are different. What separates us truly is our exposures, our assumptions and what we allow others to project on us. But I bet you found a few things from my past that's relatable to your story. We might come from different cultures or have different experiences but, at the core, we relate!

Life Has No Remote - Get Up & Change It Yourself!

Is there something I need to adjust with my Tax Exemptions to better serve my financial standing? This question/concept should be revisited at least once a year. One of the best times for this review is when you review your credit report.

In business, I have encountered quite a few folks who really don't understand what the tax exemptions on their federal and state forms mean. That's unfortunate. If the school system did not teach you this, YOU must teach yourself. Stop just filling out forms in a manner that isn't a service to you. Study to understand so that if there is a more appropriate manner, use it, pleeease!

In the beginning, I struggled in the above areas. In fact, I got an F on those tests too! While it felt like most of my classmates were winning, here I was staring at a big old flag-an 'F'in failure!

Guess what??? Here is the best news of all: it

was just a test! No, it actually was REAL life, but you get to learn and make it a teachable moment. You don't have to sulk, feel inferior or hope for extra credit.

Never give a distraction the power to become an interruption in your journey.

Now, back to your future.

See, I have lived long enough now to know that experience is an educator and greater equalizer. What do I mean by this? Well, when you really think about it, those are the "life lessons" that equip us the most. Life is REALITY! YOUR life is YOUR reality so I encourage you to do similar to what I have done. It's how I still do today. I take those life lessons and dissect them.

7. Life Lesson Format

My life lessons are broken down like this:

My Practical, Relevant

&

Real Life-Lesson Format

I. **What I thought would happen**

II. **Why I thought it would happen a particular way**

III. **What actually went right**

IV. **What went not-so-right (teachable moment)**

V. **What I will do differently next time**

VI. **Life will always present YOU a next time (be prepared for it)!**

This is my simple thought process that continues to work for me when I face any obstacle.

Real life isn't solely based on how well of a test taker you are. It's based on how well you apply what you have learned from day-to-day experiences and education (often times masking as "mistakes").

Consider this: textbook knowledge and life experiences are not one in the same. However, I think it's midway between traditional (textbook education) and non-traditional (life) education that we often find our true strength and pathway to personal sUccess.

For me, this is a level of life's playing field in most instances. So be resilient! Keep your focus! Have a sensible plan and stick to it, even when you are thrown off track from time to time.

Keep your focus! Believe me, the 20-year-old me is glad I did!

The greatest inhibitors of human progress are a toxic infatuation with one's comfort zone and uncommunicated expectations. PERIOD!

My HBCU Blues

I was 19 years old and remember vividly sitting in one of Dr. Jackson's lectures. I was excited, and somewhat intimidated, by her regal and charismatic classroom flow.

I can't quite recall the topic, all I can see is her almost cavalierly gliding in front of the classroom, every so often coughing into a handkerchief (she always carried a handkerchief). She was a stickler about being punctual and, on this particular day, I was delayed. I had worked overnight at the hospital and ended up working over.

I had transferred to this university as a soon-to-be daddy! Working/making money was a necessity. Although it wasn't the ideal situation, my "lil main man" was the priority! My girlfriend and I agreed to make every decision necessary to secure his early pilgrimage and we did just that. I didn't always get it right, however, I sacrificed and creatively tried to carve out a life at the same time. (I didn't always get that right either!)

I had a decent job at the hospital, signed my lease to my first apartment and bought furniture (from this nice lady I worked with who happened to be getting a divorce and wanted EVERYTHING GONE. That sign went right over my head! I was just glad to have a furnished apartment for my son).

The light bill was due and I needed to pick up some diapers. Due to my baby boy not being able to hold down milk, I also had to pick up more cans of… what was that milk my girlfriend said before class?

"Mr. Gholson!"

I came out of my thoughts to see to Dr. Jackson's statuesque frame tapping the corner of the podium in front of me.

"Yes?"

Dr. Jackson stared in her own space and walked away, requesting I meet her in her office on the next during work study.

My girlfriend Ti'Juana was always able to coordinate and map out plans. I was the people person and the crisis resolver! We had a system. Ti'Juana has also transferred to this university to be much closer to home and closer to our support system. We were trying to complete this traditional education track the best we knew how and with limited resources in a small town.

We often laugh about how we would schedule our classes so that we could transfer the watch of our son during class breaks to save money. I worked overnight and went to school during the day, both full time!

Ti'Juana was a full-time college student and a server at a couple of restaurants during the evenings. We had a plan and the plan was working pretty well until I started having headaches.

After some time with them not going away, I went to my doctor and his diagnosis was a 21-year-old on the verge of a heart attack caused by exhaustion. Of course, I knew it was all stress related! Ti'Juana and I were determined not to be a statistic so "we" pressed on! (I said "we" because it was a while before I even revealed to Ti'Juana that I had gone to the doctor.)

There's so much more I could tell you, but let's just say there was a chain of events that occurred after this. A chain of events including eviction, temp agency work and all sorts of car problems! I tell you what, I would never want to repeat my 20s again! I learned way more than I wanted to during that period than any other phase. There is so much more I could tell you about those lessons learned, but I'll save it for another book. Just know that my journey has been real and true.

So the time had come to go to Dr. Jackson's office. I had been there a few times before for some assignments. She really liked me. In fact, many of the professors there liked us and were rooting for our success as they watched our story unfold in real time. And our story was no fantasy. Our reality show was full of work–the work required for me to become me, support Ti'Juana and make sure our son and soon-to-arrive daughter were okay.

"Mr. Gholson, you cannot continue on in this manner, sir. The probability of your success is compromised in every way when you lack focus and cannot remain your alert self."

"I cannot tell you what your resolve will be, Mr. Gholson, but what I do know is that there will have to be one soon. I hope you are understanding what is being said to you, sir. I applaud you for your ambition, however, it may best serve you in some alternative manner."

Dr. Jackson had such a way with words but, trust me, I understood exactly what she was saying. Looking back, in a special way she was freeing me to free me! I think she recognized I was no quitter and to stop was to admit defeat.

My alternative? I saw a recruiter and did well on my test. The recruiter told me that I could make more money if we got married before I joined the military. Out of left field, I made the smoothest proposal known to man. (Lol, you will have read Ti'Juana's book, *Girl What you Gonna Do with Your Money?* for the exact words and how I proposed. It was a proposal for the books.)

Ti'Juana hugged me and said… Yes! Well, I'll share this from her book, her response was more like: *You ain't leaving me in Petersburg with two kids.* She and I have always lived in the non-traditional zone, trust me. Yet, we always had a plan.

My wife and I have consistently taken the path less chosen to achieve our goals. Unconventional routes and detours are not the enemy! Remember, as I share throughout this book, sometimes the best lessons come from unlearning stuff that doesn't serve you! What may have worked for Uncle Billy and PaPa Earnest back in the day may never work for you and that's okay. Actually, that's normal!

The world has changed. You are different and your expectations are different. Even though your basic life needs are the same, like me, you may find that you have to move differently due to current social and economic constructs. I know that is what I had to do.

Financial strategies are often generationally driven and that's okay. So don't continue doing yourself a disservice by traveling a route if it doesn't provide for you or progress you. If the route is not leading you to where you desire to be then I challenge you to revisit my personal life-lesson format in this workbook.

Another amazing reality about this "canvas of life and learning cycle" is this: I now get the awesome opportunity to travel and speak with college students (many with stories similar to mine). I am able to demonstrate hope and identify, relate to and share my truth along my journey. And, yes, even on that same campus of my HBCU blues, I get to be the difference maker–my own version of Dr. Jackson!

So, once again, I ask you:

Are you willing to stop living the life you have now in order to live the life you want?

8. Life with No Training Wheels

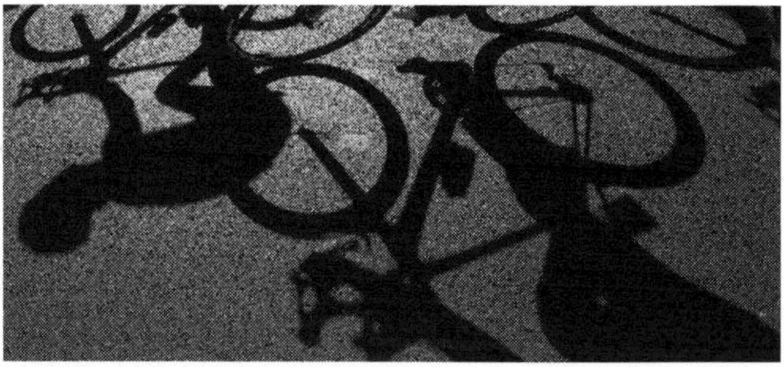

"You can do this grandson and I'm not gonna let you quit!"

"I know you're mad and frustrated, but PaPop told you that we were gonna learn how to ride this bike with NO training wheels this summer, young sir! Stop being afraid to fall! You are gonna fall at first, we all do. It's okay!"

My 5-year-old grandson looks up at me, with frustrated red cheeks and watery eyes, and says, "Okay, PaPop." It's almost enough to make me cave in, but I needed him to believe in himself and in his process as much as I believed in him.

Over a year and a half before, his Nana and I bought him and his brother bikes. We were so excited to witness that little gleam of joy when they saw the bikes. Like any grandparent, they melt us with their every smile.

The boys jumped up and down wildly, hugging and thanking us. All was right with our world. My 7-year-old grandson learned how to ride that summer. He is the happy-go-lucky kid, very energetic and driven. So for him it was simply going to happen, despite the falls, bruises or fear. As long as he knew PaPop was nearby to help him, he was perfectly cool as a cucumber.

Not my "baby boy", (my nickname for Ro'Mir, my middle grandson). See, one of those special things I love about baby boy is that he does not succumb to peer pressure. Though competitive like his big brother, he does not have the drive to prove anything, he simply shows up with his very own level of cool confidence and a healthy ego. (He kind of reminds me of me and my approach to life).

So despite his brother's motivation to rise above his fears of falling or failing, I knew that would never serve as an antidote for baby boy. No, PaPop had to strategize and build on that strategy over time.

Throughout the first year with these little bikers, I observed my oldest grandson take his confidence level to all sorts of heights.

"Look at me, PaPop!" He was able to scale down the steepest hill with no fear or falls.

"Look at me, PaPop!" He strengthened his leg muscles and was able to pedal up those same steep hills where he once had to stop at some point and push his bike the rest of the way.

"Oh yay, look at my 'lil main man'"! ("Lil main man" was Lawrence III's nickname for my grandson, also known as "3"). 3 had overcome and mastered much fear in this short time. I celebrated and encouraged him all along the way. When he needed me, PaPop was there!

So I watched and strategized. With all the mastering lil main man did, baby boy still cautiously put on his elbow and knee pads and helmet. He would slowly and haphazardly pedal along, with training wheels in tow. On the surface, he appeared unbothered, but I knew him and his brother knew him too.

Baby boy wanted to appear brave and compete with his big brother, so he disguised his fear of falling with a cocky I-don't-care-about-all-of-that attitude. My game plan had to be a time released carefully orchestrated thing for this young king!

IGNORANCE is not bliss! As MEN dealing with money matters, every day we have to become okay with daily educating ourselves. After all, you, my friend, are a BUSINESS!

You are a creative force filled with potential and unlimited possibilities that those in your world depend on. You have a commodity: *something of value that can be sold, bought or exchanged due to supply and demand.* If that alone doesn't make you stand tall, square your shoulders, hold your head up high and make a resounding roar, nothing else will!

Now, if you choose to act that last sentence out, I suggest you do it in the privacy of your home. I would hate to see your self-affirming moment be misinterpreted as some type of mental breakdown, ha-ha!

We are men, see us roar and soar, forevermore! (Feels good, right!?)

Men, encourage yourself: embrace your significance, live boldly in your own truth and in your own light!

Seriously, managing or self-managing our financial livelihood really is like running a business and like riding a bike, eventually with no training wheels. You have to focus on the purpose, the process, the potential and the productivity! This means building your own brand of confidence so that you can maneuver and understand the language of money that is a part of everyday life.

It's all around us guys and there is no escaping dealing with it, so it's best to be prepared. Anything that involves your money should definitely be seen as something that is worthy of your attention and time. Don't you dare to continue to get lost in the journey *because it doesn't make sense to me, I am going to ignore it* syndrome. We all know that it's only through practice that we get better. Hopefully, once we know better, we do better.

Understanding what I call "the language of money", results in our ability to make better decisions, especially when it comes to which types of services or products we choose. Before I continue, let me say that I know what you're thinking:

> *"Lawrence, you make this shit sound easy, but I get headaches just thinking about it!"*

But, by now, you already know what I am going to ask you, right?

Are you willing to stop living the life you have now in order to live the life you want?

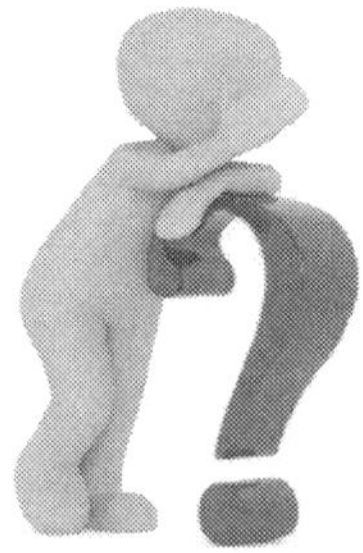

Man, I will not sit here and tell you the bald-faced lie that it starts out easy! I will not tell you that you will always get it right. But I will tell you that it becomes easier the more you focus and face it. Just like working out target muscle groups, it is hard in the begining and your body feels all sorts of pains. Oh, the pain, the pain, the PAIN! Yet, if you remain consistent with that workout regimen, you will see results that you will be happy about.

See, we have trained ourselves to overcome the physical pain of working out and remain focused on the desired outcome. Or, maybe, like my older grandson who eventually was able to ride his bike all the way to the top of the hill instead of having to get off and push it the rest of the way, we become stronger simply because it makes more sense to us. Really, what we did was harness control over our workout habits, our eating habits and our muscle memory for the WIN!

It's when we don't open the mail, or when it's stuffed in the stack of I-will-open-it-SOME-day pile, it's in those moments that we decide to let money control us.

See how I tied all of that up in there? It's amazing how a seemingly simple everyday activity like riding a bike or, more specifically, learning to ride a bike with no training wheels, has layers of practical life lessons when we really consider them.

In that beautiful summer moment, my grandson needed coaching to propel him to overcome and excel. He may not have even understood the importance of it at that moment, perhaps due to frustration, uncertainty and even pride. But I knew he needed to succeed in order to "level up". The old adage "just like riding a bike" really is true and the real honest truth is that the process is different (although beneficial) for everyone brave enough to not quit their sUccess. That summer, baby boy walked into his truth!

As a demonstrational, "add value" coach, I see many "baby boy" scenarios, especially among men when it comes to minding our money! Trust me, the level of education, expertise or professional success has little impact on how men approach these nuances of life. I know this path all too well, especially with unlearning, relearning, delaying gratification, overcoming fear and failure. The things we say to ourselves can be crushing–no one's expectations of us impact us more than our own. Isn't that correct, fellas?

I have fought this dragon – (sometimes demon and other times Goliath) – throughout my financial journey. I haven't always won either! But I never quit and I treated each and every fight as my teachable moment.

Today, I can say that I am always winning. The battles have not stopped, necessarily, but I know how to fight the battle. I also know my inclinations and internal battles as well as the nature of M-O-N-E-Y. I heard money's voice, listened to what it had to say and responded.

So, I know there are at least two questions you have for me:

- **WHAT DID I DO?**
- **HOW DID I DO IT?**

Turn the page, my brother.

MIND ON MY MONEY!!!

A Thinking Man's Journal on Money Matters

Well, it all started with my mindset, more like a Mindset Change! Unlearning what no longer served me and learning what did. I guess you can safely say that I saw the value in investing in ME first. I had to start with the way I thought about money and being brave enough to learn its language.

Simply put, I now have My Mind on My Money! So, again, I ask you sir/bro/bruh/broski/brotha/brother man/dude:

Are you willing to stop living the life you have now in order to live the life you want????

For me, minding my money all started with this one practical, relevant and real question. Answering this one question opened the door to my self-discovery.

Seek Knowledge and Apply Daily

My suggestion, in BIG BOLD Print, is that you simply start with educating yourself. Start identifying the impact of money on your daily life. You will be amazed at how much self-education you gain in this simple process.

This is where we must start! Shift out of park, gear up into drive guys and get going! Even if you are not certain of what roadblocks or delays lie ahead of you, you do know where you intend on going. Educate yourself through reading, asking questions, attending networking events or seminars and even observing your spending habits and those of others. You, alone, establish or reestablish your money habits and money beliefs.

I have acquired quite a few friends who are well-versed in financial matters and wealth strategies. I make it a habit to sit down and talk with them. Sometimes we meet at their office or mine; other times we catch up over lunch. I encourage you to do the same. Not only will you learn a thing or two, but you may actually develop unexpected friendships along the way. As you build on these relationships, you become more comfortable with asking questions.

People love to share their knowledge and, who knows, you may just find out about networks, phone apps or great programs you may qualify for to help you with managing your money?

Even simple internet searches on financial terms will provide you amazing insight. Just free your mind to expand your knowledge of money. Keep doing this over and over and one day, you will be more comfortable in conversations about money. On that day, you will not only understand the language of money, but you will also be able to speak it!

DO NOT let fear or pride cause you to not grow or succeed. Many struggle with the subject of money management (also known as spending habits). It's okay to acknowledge that, fellas, but then you must decide to be better and move on. See, I get to be the fly on the wall sometimes with my clients, so I can assure you that the whole macho *I-already-*

know crap hinders us from actually learning or growing.

Here is some basic language we should all be familiar with that my wife provides in her book, *Girl, What you Gonna do with Your Money?*:

Money Management Checklist

- **Check your insurance.** Many Americans are either underinsured or over-insured. Make sure that you regularly check your insurance policies for adequate coverage and correct pricing.
- **Check your interest rates.** Regularly check your interest rates and negotiate with creditors to reduce rates whenever possible.
- **Review your credit score annually.** Take advantage of printing your free credit report each year. Pull all three at:

  www.annualcreditreport.com

- **Devise a strategy to pay your debts down.** Plan a strategy to pay your debts down regularly until they are paid in full.
- **Know your debt to income ratio (and reduce it as much as possible).** Start by writing down what you bring in and what's going out.

Money Management Checklist (continued)

- **Know your spending habits.** Keep track of what you spend by writing it down and saving receipts. At the end of each day/week total your expenditures. Look at your receipts to see what you spend the most money on.
- **Learn about the investment market.** Google information to educate yourself. Attend free classes at your bank.
- **Take advantage of free money.** If you work for someone, check to see if the company offers a company match for each dollar you invest (or a specified amount)? Take advantage of it.
- **Establish a retirement plan.** If you work for someone, take advantage of any offered retirement plans that work for you. If you own a business, create your exit strategy. Too many of the self-employed do not establish a retirement plan. This is even more important when you don't work for someone else.
- **Know your retirement figure and date.** Whether employed or self-employed, you need to know how much money is necessary for you to retire at the age you want to retire. Once you know that figure, you can devise a plan to create the cash flow that will take care of you when you are no longer able to actively work or run your business.

- **Have an emergency fund.** The standard is at least six to twelve months of your wages in your savings account for emergencies.

Gentleman, I tried to keep this as honest and practical as possible. There are some deeper areas, but that comes with time like anything else. Just like Steve, the mechanic guy, I can only help you when I know your story. But, equally like my grandson, I am here to tell you that YOU can do life without training wheels and there are awesome resources available to help you get there.

Depending on where your GPS locates you along this journey to minding your money, you will be able to identify the lane leading to your destination. Jump in, buckle up, start your engine, shift into drive and get going! Where you exit is up to you. How far you go, is up to you, just know that you are more than capable of "securing your bag" and enjoying your success journey.

It's not a vision until the ink dries.

When your money is funny, nothing else is.

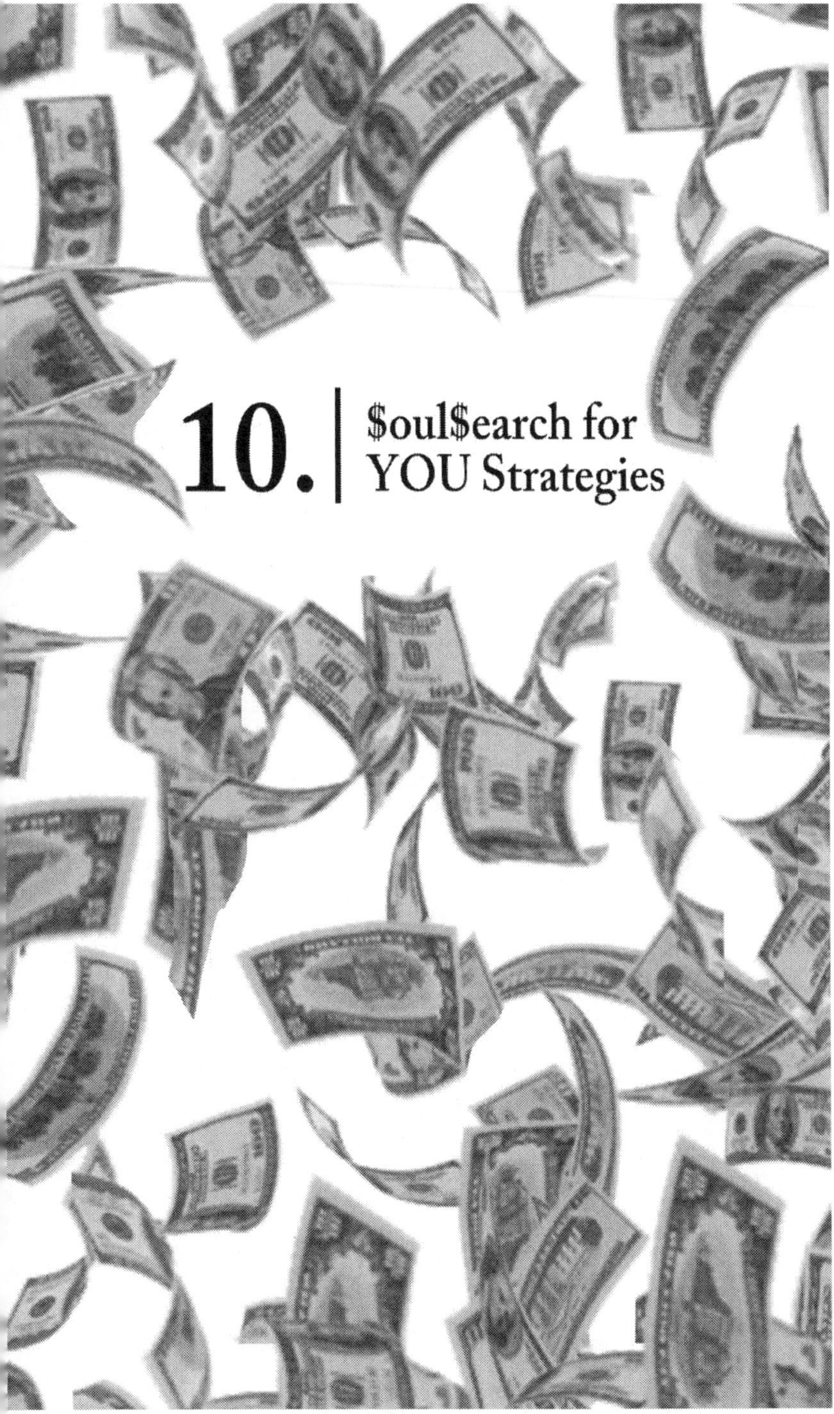

10. oulearch for YOU Strategies

This part of the workbook is what I call your **oulearch for YOU $trategies**. It's only intended to be a suggestive guide that YOU alone write out, YOU alone decide and YOU alone wholeheartedly commit to doing for YOU!

What is your Why for your MONEY?

____

____

____

Who do you know who represents your idea of success? Why?

____

____

____

What are the secrets of his/her success? Have you asked him/her?* Why or Why not?

____

____

____

*If you have not asked him or her, I encourage you to do so. Text them, message them or invite them to brunch or something. ASK!

In my experience, most successful people enjoy sharing, you just have to schedule the interaction on purpose. (Now, I don't mean be creepy and stalk them, but wholeheartedly ASK or make your request known.)

How do you plan to achieve his/her level of success?

____

____

____

____

____

Have you shared your success goals? What has been the response?

____

____

____

____

____

How are these responses impacting your thought process?

11. oulearch for YOU Journal

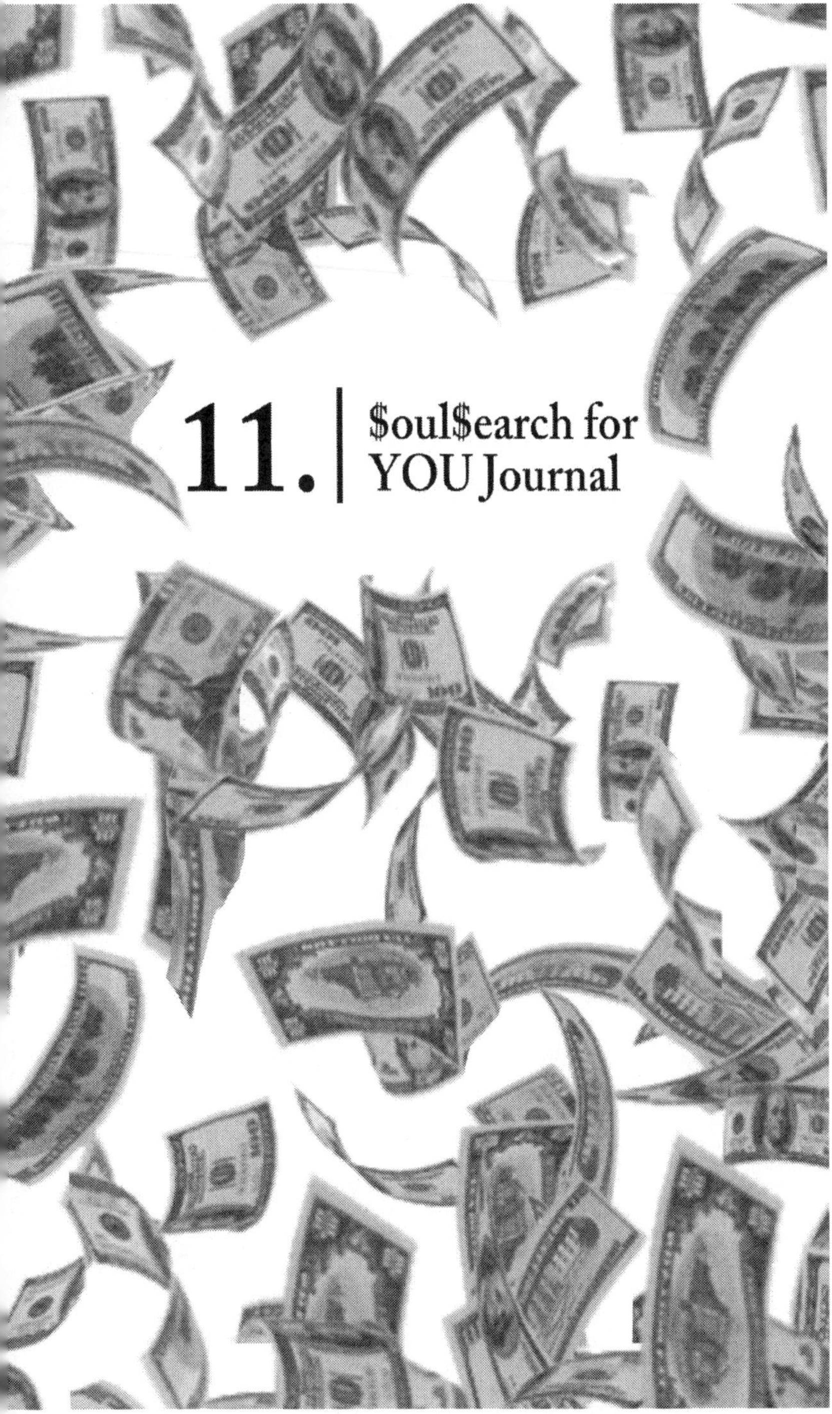

oulearch for YOU Journal

Now, I need to motivate you to actually do what you just read instead of just reading. You may not be able to control everything you confront in life, but you can always control your effort.

oulearch for YOU Journal

(No more journal lines–they inhibit your thought process. Write, draw and scribble with retaining the information in mind.)

SIDE NOTE: I can tell by the length of time it takes you to do anything whether you are going to do ANYTHING!

oulearch for YOU Journal

Refrain from misidentifying a part of your process as the final destination along your journey. You are forever in metamorphosis. Red Lights only give you rest while you anticipate your Green Lights of LIFE.

oulearch for YOU Journal

Unharnessed anger can be dangerous & debilitating. We must learn to channel our anger and use it to propel us to make great decisions.

MIND ON MY MONEY!!!

A Thinking Man's Journal on Money Matters

oulearch for YOU Journal

News flash: you got *here* and that's good, but please know that what got you *here* cannot take you *there*. Get uncomfortable!

oulearch for YOU Journal

I have now come to know that Disappointments & Hard Times don't come to stay. NOPE, they come to pass so remain uncomfortable during the turbulence of life, but STAY ENCOURAGED!

What life changes have impacted your success?

How have you adjusted? Have you lost momentum, pressed on or just given up?

oulearch for YOU Journal

What support do you need? Honestly, have you asked for it?

____________________ ____________________

____________________ ____________________

____________________ ____________________

____________________ ____________________

It's okay to challenge your beliefs!

If you believe what you were told about money and its working for you, keep it! If not, throw it out! It's as simple as that. But if you never take or make the time to do this, you may find yourself always struggling with money despite any level of success you achieve.

ABOUT THE AUTHOR

Lawrence A. Gholson II is a certified team building facilitator, demonstrational life-coach and speaker.

With an urban approach, Lawrence provides mentorship and coaching to small business owners, contract professionals and teams through his company YOU FACTOR COACHING. He brings over twenty years' experience in professional and personal development, diversity training and organizational strategy.

Specializing in creative partnerships and synergizing winning teams, he challenges you to maximize every teachable moment in order to achieve your goals and ultimately discover your better self. He calls it the discovery of your YOU Factor!

Lawrence A. Gholson II

Hey folks, I would love to connect with you and your vision! I'm an inspiring, encouraging and motivating speaker, but my #1 goal is to ADD VALUE through demonstrational and practical exchange. This goal requires challenging YOU to access, dissect and strategize current opportunities before you and liberating YOU to access, dissect and strategize who you need to become at your *here* in order to arrive at your *there*.

I enjoy creating Team Building Think Tanks as well as professional speaking and adding value to your Success Journey.

"sUccess is YOUniversal"

let's Connect!

Get your FREE 10-minute phone session!

www.lawrencegholson.com

Join our social media community!

Y O U Factor Coaching on INSTAGRAM

@YourMAXIMIZEDlife on FACEBOOK

Made in the USA
Columbia, SC
23 November 2021

49627172R00076